Four Seasons of Top-Bar Beekeeping

Print Edition

A Zip Gun Guide

This is a 'Zip Gun Guide'. It is not intended to be a huge, scholarly encyclopedia like you'd find in the dusty far reaches of the public library. It is short and to the point and it is written by someone with (figuratively) dirty hands. As with a zip gun (that might fire a bullet when built correctly, but could explode in your hand when not), please apply common sense and good judgment before applying the suggestions herein.

Dedication

Thanks go to Debra, and my mom.

*Without their encouragement, suggestions,
and patient reading and re-reading,
there would be little here.*

Contents

Introduction

With the news media's oft repeated, dire, stories about "colony collapse disorder", or perhaps just as a fad, there has been a renewed interest in beekeeping across the world. Urban locations are seeing odd hives pop up here and there, and in more rural areas it's becoming a rare day one can take a drive and not see a hive or two.

Maybe it's the sweet golden goodness; but honey bees, it seems, are a creature we don't want to see disappear. This guide is for budding apiarists (beekeepers) who, like the author, want to ease themselves into hobby beekeeping using a top-bar hive.

At the time of writing, the author and his bees are living in the USA, so while much of this guide should be of use to readers worldwide, it may occasionally become slightly US-centric.

Please note – this guide is not intended to replace a good book on beekeeping or the diseases of bees, merely offer some suggestions specific to top-bar beekeeping that may not be covered. Also it is said that if 15 beekeepers discuss something there will be at least 16 opinions on how it should be done.

 FUN FACT
A clay jar containing honey was discovered in King Tut's tomb when it was explored in 1922. Despite being over 2000 years old, it was still good to eat.

Prologue
(a winter without bees)

The first decision to make when considering beekeeping is to evaluate where you could keep a hive, and then what type of hive you think it should be. With those decisions made, you can build a list of the materials and tools you'll need.

Before you do any shopping though, I'd advise you search for local beekeeping clubs and events. Attend a beginners seminar if you can. Even though many seasoned beekeepers may think top-bar hives are a crazy idea, they will normally still be willing to share advice regarding local conditions and sources of bees.

In the US at least, many regional beekeeping clubs offer free or inexpensive one- or two-day introductory sessions, and some community and technical colleges offer short (6 or 8 week) courses of evening classes. While these will probably be geared toward removable frame hives, they are an excellent source of information, advice, contacts, and very often bee suppliers. Package bees are generally ordered in the January/February time-frame (sometimes earlier) for installation after the last frost, and the sessions generally coincide with the order taking window.

Before you buy anything else, buy a recent book about beekeeping (or two, or three, ...) and read it. There are also many, many, older books available that are out of copyright[1] but still have have excellent general advice – they will however be hopelessly out of date with regards to

---

1   CDs and DVDs collections go for a few dollars on eBay.

parasites, diseases and their treatments.

Inside a hive

The hive is a colony of bees. Everything the bees do is for the good of the colony, driven by communal instinct. Sometimes it will seem that the colony itself is like a living creature and the individuals within the collective are just components of the whole.

Inside a hive you will find adult bees, the comb they build from beeswax, brood (eggs and larvae in the comb), food stores (pollen and nectar/honey) and propolis (a sticky resin found on tree buds used to seal the hive). There are three types of adult bee; queens (usually one per hive), drones and workers.

 The queen exists to lay eggs (she can lay up to 2,000 eggs, or twice her own body weight, per day). She is longer than the workers and drones and is usually found somewhere around the brood comb. She does not actively direct the workers, but they are responsive to her pheromones. It is the workers however who decide if and when she is to be replaced.

 Male drones exist only to mate with a new queen (usually from a different hive), and will die if successful. They have larger eyes (to spot a queen on her mating flight) and are heavier set than the workers, but have no stinger. In the fall they tend to be driven out of the hive as an unnecessary drain on its resources.

4

The female workers make up the bulk of the colony. They provide food for the queen, the eggs she has laid and the larvae that hatch. When young they clean the hive and secrete 'royal jelly' which is fed to the larvae[2]. Later they

secrete beeswax, and use it to build the hexagonal cells of comb, before progressing to roles of accepting pollen and nectar from foragers, and placing it in storage cells (where the stored nectar converts into honey). Finally they become foragers themselves, collecting nectar, pollen and propolis. An average worker will only produce $\frac{1}{12}$th teaspoon of honey in her lifetime.

Choosing your hive type

Basic mud and clay hives, log gums and and woven grass or straw skeps are still in use in some parts of the world, but do not allow inspection of the bees so are a no-go in the USA and many other countries where laws explicitly prohibit their use or require access for disease/pest control. In the developed world, hives such as the Langstroth, 'National' and 'Commercial' types (and their derivatives) are by far the most common with removable frames guiding the construction of comb and allowing honey to be extracted mechanically. In other parts of the world, top-bar hives are the norm due to their simplicity, and a growing number of hobbyists are starting out with a top-bar hive. (There is also

---

2   Royal jelly is fed to all larvae for the first three days, but only to prospective new queens thereafter – drone and worker larvae are switched to a diet of honey and pollen.

a sort of removable frame/top-bar hybrid called the Warré or "Peoples Hive" that offers many of the benefits of both removable frame and top-bar hives.)

Wikipedia has an excellent description of the various types of beehive available[3].

From left to right: a Langstroth Hive, a Kenyan Top-Bar Hive, and the Author.
(Debra Anderson)

 FUN FACT
Native Americans called the honeybee "White Man's Flies" after Europeans imported the honeybee in the 17th Century.

---

3   https://en.wikipedia.org/wiki/Beehive

The following tables compare Top-Bar and Langstroth hives.

Top-Bar Hive	Removable Frame Hive
Modern top-bar hives are an incremental improvement over older traditional methods.	Rev. Lorenzo Langstroth developed his hive in the 1850's based on $^3/_8$-in. "bee space".
A trough shaped container with removable *top bars*.	A set of, one or more, stacked wooden boxes containing removable *frames*.
The bee colony expands horizontally along the trough managing their own brood and honey storage.	The beekeeper keeps the queen and brood in the lowest box and stacks additional boxes for surplus honey.
Comb built 'free form' along top bars with no side supports.	Bees build comb over wax or plastic template in removable frames.
 Fully built out comb on a top-bar (Debra Anderson)	 Clean foundation in a Langstroth frame (Debra Anderson)
Harvesting involves removal of honey **and** comb.	Harvesting generally involves extraction of honey from comb allowing reuse of comb.

The Bottom Line...	
+ Cheaper to start-up – a home built hive can be made with few tools and scrap lumber.	– Multiple components required – some purchases can be delayed but are required eventually.
– No real standards.	+ Standardized, interchangeable equipment
+ Less on-going maintenance.	– Requires frequent inspection.
– Less productive.	+ Efficient, almost 'industrial', honey production.
– Fewer off-the-shelf solutions.	+ Multiple Internet and mail-order vendors.
If you are looking to have pollinators in your garden, with maybe a little honey as a bonus, and would rather let the bees manage themselves; a top-bar hive may be appropriate.	If you want to produce honey in any quantity, and have the time to manage the hive, a Langstroth type hive is probably the better choice.

 FUN FACT
It takes roughly 2 million flower visits, with over 55,000 miles flown, to produce a single pound of honey.

Selecting a spot

Whatever type of hive you chose you are going to have to put it **somewhere**. As no two situations are identical I will suggest criteria to judge possible locations.

- Are the bees entering and leaving the hive going to bother people? Be aware of your neighbors and children – don't create a perceived or real hazard.
- Will it be protected from high winds?
- Will it offer some shade in the summer?
- Will it flood or fill with snow drifts?
- Can **you** get to it easily all year?
- Is there food and water nearby?
- A South or East facing position is often best.

Bees are fairly adaptable and will fly a couple of miles from the hive to gather food, but excessive travel, extremes of temperature and high winds should be avoided.

Refining the choice

Having researched the topic and decided that top-bar beekeeping is for you, the first step is to buy or build your hive. At its simplest, your hive is a trough-like box with a removable lid, an entry hole (or holes) and a series of removable horizontal strips (top bars) running across the shorter dimension, from which comb can hang. Generally 18 – 20 top bars is considered appropriate.

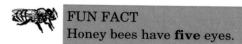

FUN FACT
Honey bees have **five** eyes.

Top-bar hives can be broken down into three basic types:

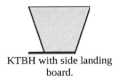

KTBH with side landing board.

Kenyan (aka KTBH) – a wooden trough with sloping sides form a V shape with a flat bottom. The angle between the base and side is generally between 100° and 120°. Conventional wisdom suggests that the bees are less likely to join comb to the sides, but there is much dispute as to if this is true, let alone what angle might be optimal.

Tanzanian hive with front landing board.

Tanzanian – similar to the Kenyan hive but with vertical sides (i.e. a 90° angle between base and side). Because there are no angled cuts, it is considered easier to build than the Kenyan hive.

"Honey Cow"

Creative designs – one off and unusual solutions. An example of such is the "Honey Cow"[4] which is constructed from a 55-gallon food-grade storage barrel cut in half. The pouring holes are used as entrances.

It is common, but not universal, for the the bottom to be extended along one side as a landing board, on both the Kenyan and Tanzanian style hives. Either a short or a long side may be extended. Holes or a slot for the hive entrance are generally cut immediately above the landing board. When there is no landing board, the entrance may be at any convenient point.

---

4   http://www.velacreations.com/honeycow.html

Also, it is worth noting that most Langstroth hive beekeepers have moved to using wire mesh, rather than solid wooden bottoms to their hives. This improves ventilation, but more significantly appears to reduce Verroa mite populations. When first introduced, your bees will want a very dark hive, so if you do use a screened bottom, you should also consider some sort of light-block cover – at least until they are established.

Whatever the hive style, it is best to raise the hive off the ground using a stand of some sort.

Top Bars

Top bars themselves are generally $1\frac{1}{4}$" - $1\frac{3}{8}$" (32mm – 35mm) wide, with a length sufficient to overhang both side walls. The width range is chosen to provide adequate spacing between the wax combs that will hang down from them. The height should be enough to support several lbs of suspended honeycomb without bending.

In order to direct the construction of comb, the bars should either taper (below left), or have a slot cut into which molten wax is poured (below center), or a wooden strip is glued[5] (below right).

Different Top-Bar Profiles

---

5   If you elect to use this style, be aware that the unfilled ends of the slot can provide a hiding place for small hive beetle.

Getting Ready

When the flowers start blooming, bees can start foraging. Sellers of bee packages generally schedule things so package bees go out when food becomes available. In the weeks between ordering your bees and their availability get ready...

Position your hive in its intended location ahead of time (see 'Selecting a spot' above).

Gather your tools – a bee suit, hive tool and smoker are not essential to top-bar beekeeping, but are advised. A plastic spray bottle will be needed to install your bee package. You will also, most likely, need some form of syrup feeder.

Prepare the sugar water for the spray bottle and the syrup you will need to augment their feeding (see 'Bee Food - Spring').

Other considerations

Consider the fact that you will be stung - it is an inevitable part of beekeeping; and while for most people it is a painful annoyance[6], there is always the risk of an allergic reaction, possibly severe. (If stung always scrape the stinger out with a flat edge – don't use tweezers and squeeze more venom into the wound.)

There are many places that enforce restrictions on locations of hives and beekeeping – make yourself aware of any

---

6   As the beekeeper's body desensitizes to the bee venom, it is common for stings to become progressively less painful and the reaction less severe.

laws, bylaws, covenants and ordinances that will apply to you.

The Internet can be your friend. Research beekeeping in general and top-bar keeping specifically – be sure both are for you before spending your hard earned money.

 FUN FACT
Honey is sweeter than table sugar.

Spring

With luck the flowers will be in bloom and there will be no more frosts when you collect your bees. It is an exciting day, but try to stay calm and work methodically.

Installing a Bee Package

A package of bees waiting to be installed.

 FUN FACT
Lighter honeys have milder flavors, while the darker colors are stronger.

14

Requirements:

- A top bar hive (20 bars assumed).
- A hive divider - a board to temporarily seal off the back half of the hive.
- A 2lb or 3lb bee **package**[7].
- A feeder containing 1:1 syrup (see 'Bee Food - Spring' later). This can be a standard entrance feeder clamped to your landing board or something you fashion yourself[8].
- A spray bottle containing sugar water (1 sugar: 4 water), <u>not</u> 1:1 syrup.
- A short length of wire.
- A bee suit (recommended).

Hive awaiting the package

---

7   "Nucs" (nucleus hives) are already installed in Langstroth style frames and are unlikely to be compatible with your hive.

8   When I installed my first package I initially used a food jar that had a rectangular opening and cut a strip of hardware cloth to sit diagonally across the contents so the bees would not get stuck in the syrup. This was placed inside the hive. Losses were not great, but refilling was problematic. I quickly switched to an entrance feeder.

Installation:
1. Suit up if you have a bee suit.

2. Remove the hive lid.

3. If you have a slot entrance, partially block the hive entrance with your restrictor, (or grass or straw), so only one or two bees can get through at a time. If you have multiple hole entrances, cork all but one. Reducing access will make it easier for your bees to protect themselves for the first few days.

4. Remove the first 9 bars and insert the hive divider between bars 10 and 11 - this is not essential but encourages the bees to build their brood comb at the front of the hive.

An open hive showing a 'false back' hive divider at around bar 10.

5. Replace bars 1 through 5 and, after a gap, 6 – we will put the queen cage between 5 and 6.

16

6. Carefully spray the bees with sugar water, avoiding the queen, and tap the package on the ground to bump the loose bees down.

7. Remove the queen cage from the package (ensuring the other bees cannot escape), and follow the packagers instructions - usually removing a piece of tape or cork to expose a candy plug. **Do not remove the candy plug.**

Examine the queen cage – there are several designs in use, some plastic and some wooden. If the cage contains two or three attendants in addition to the queen – be sure to place the opening upward so that an attendant will not block the queen's way out if she dies.

8. Suspend the queen cage between bars 5 and 6 (so it will not easily fall) using some wire to temporarily hold it in place if you have to - you will be removing it in a couple of days.

9. Spray the remaining bees with more sugar water and 'bump down' the package until they are pretty much all clumped together in the bottom of the package.

10. Remove the feeding can and empty the package into the front of the hive - tap the package to try to get all the bees into the hive

11. Replace bars 6 through 9.
If there is a spare bar because of the false back and queen cage, hold onto it for later.

12. Replace the hive lid.

13. Pour the syrup from the feeding can into your feeder and top off with your prepared syrup.

Queen cage in place and bees emptied into hive body.

Monitoring

Two or three days after installation, you are going to have to check the hive. Fire up your smoker[9] and wear your bee suit – your bees are probably not going to be especially calm yet.

Remove the hive lid and gently separate bars 5 and 6 (you may have to remove a later bar and shuffle the bars down to make enough room). The bee cluster is probably centered around the queen cage, pulling several bars (centered around 5 and 6) together – use a little smoke and don't worry too much about bees coming out of the opening. Carefully remove the queen cage and check that the queen

---

9   Not that it will do much good until the bees have started making honey.

has been released - there may be comb attached, so try to do as little damage as possible. If the queen is still in the cage check that the sugar plug is uncovered and make a small hole in it (taking great care not to harm the queen!) and replace the cage. Adjust the bars carefully (try not to squish any bees!) and replace the 'spare' bar if necessary. If the bees have started building comb then the hive divider can be removed if you wish - some keepers prefer to reduce the hive volume until comb is fully built out, and then expand it as necessary.

If you had to replace the queen cage, repeat again in a day or so – if at that time the queen is still not free, remove the sugar plug and allow the queen to exit and join her helpers. I cannot stress this enough – at this stage especially – look after your queen.

Over the next week or so, top off the feeder as it empties, but assuming flowers are out, don't exceed a gallon of syrup overall. The syrup feeds the bees and stimulates comb building, but we want the bees collecting nectar and pollen as soon as they are reasonably established.

Keep an eye on your hive and note the comings and goings of the bees. Let them settle in to their new home for a week or two. After that periodically check that all is well (see 'Summer' for maladies to check for) and consider feeding should there be an extended period of bad weather that prevents foraging.

Bee Food - Spring

Syrup

When first setting up the hive, and during periods the bees are active but there are little or no food supplies, you will have to feed your bees. This is normally done with a sugar and water mix called "syrup". Traditionally a 1:1 ratio[10] is used in Spring feeding and a 2 sugar : 1 water is used in Fall, however there are advocates for 5:3 or 2:1 year around. Feel free to experiment. Whatever you choose, remember to use regular white granulated sugar - the bees can't digest the impurities in brown sugar.

To make 1:1 syrup, bring one quart of water to a boil to kill any bacteria and add one quart of dry granulated sugar - stir until dissolved. Do not be surprised that 1 quart of water plus one quart of sugar yields less than 2 quarts of syrup. 2:1 syrup may require additional gentle heat to help dissolve the additional sugar.

Sugar Water

Not really 'food', but a tool to calm package bees, 1:4 sugar water is 1 part sugar to 4 parts water, made up in a manner similar to syrup. A small quantity will be needed when installing the bee package. There are commercial additives that many beekeepers swear by, while others add a drop or two of food grade lemon-grass and spearmint oils.

---

10 By some stroke of luck the densities of water and household sugar are sufficiently close that measurements can be by either weight or volume.

Grease Patty

- 1 part vegetable shortening (e.g. Crisco brand)
- 2 parts white sugar
- small amounts of mineral salt and wintergreen or tea-tree essential oils are sometimes added to this mix to reduce mite problems, however these should **never** be added leading up to honey extraction.

The constituents are blended to form a paste. Flatten it into thin sheets that can be draped-over/pushed-onto empty comb, or attached to a spare top-bar. Excess may be stored between sheets of greaseproof paper and frozen. This can be used year round – especially with essential oils for mite treatment. A basic patty (no essential oils) is belied to help reduce tracheal mite transmission.

Pollen Patties

Sugar water any syrup will provided your bees with carbohydrates, but they are also going to need protein. Provided there are flowering plants for them to forage from, they will most likely be able to fend for themselves, but it would not hurt to offer them a small amount of a commercially obtained pollen feed.

Summer

It takes a lot of bees to make a lot of honey. Over the course of her life a worker bee may produce $^{1}/_{12}$th teaspoon of honey, visiting up to 2000 flowers per day. As the sun shines and the nectar flows, your bees are should be busy collecting collecting nectar and pollen, and raising more bees. The hope is, that with at top-bar hive, the bees will pretty much manage themselves and don't need a lot of maintenance; but even a top-bar hive must be checked periodically (every couple of weeks) for strange behaviors, signs of disease, pests, parasites or other problems.

Swarming

There are many reasons a colony of bees may raise a new queen, among them is a desire to reproduce, splitting the colony in two. Somewhat more than half or the worker bees will gather with the old queen a short distance from the hive and wait while scouts search for a suitable new home, leaving any remaining brood, a new queen, and less than half of the original worker caste the old one. When a new site is found the swarm will all fly to the new location and attempt to found a new hive. The swarm may look worrisome (especially when the bees move en mass), but they are rarely aggressive. Swarms may be collected by beekeepers to start new hives.

 FUN FACT
Honeybees will visit 50 to 100 flowers on a foraging trip.

"Hive"
(Bobby Mikul - Public Domain)

Normally this is a late spring/early summer occurrence and is unlikely to happen in the first year unless the colony has outgrown the available space. Thereafter the beekeeper should consider swarm management techniques, or capture and move the swarm into a new top bar hive.

Bearding

Looking somewhat similar to the waiting stage of swarming is "bearding". On hot sticky evenings, returning bees will cluster around the entrance overnight, rather than resting within. This is not really anything to worry too much about, but may indicate that the hive is not well ventilated, or could use some shading from the sun. The obvious difference between a waiting swarm and a beard, is that the beard cluster forms on the hive rather than a short distance away.

If bearding becomes excessive, it might indicate the need for a ventilation hole to aid airflow. A ½"diameter screened[11] hole may be worth adding high on the back wall of the hive.

---

11 Window 'bug screen' mesh is perfect.

Mild bearding on a hot day.

Maladies

There are many and varied diseases, parasites and pests that can affect the health of the hive. Detection and treatment methods change frequently, and approval for use can vary by locality. A frequently updated list of issues and approved treatments is maintained by The Mid-Atlantic Apiculture Research and Extension Consortium (MAAREC) at http://maarec.psu.edu. Penn State's Collage of Agricultural Sciences also publishes an excellent "Field Guide to Honey Bees and Their Maladies".

At the time of writing the top issues effecting hive health seem to be parasites: *Verroa destructor* – an external mite that not only inherently weakens the bees, but is the vector for numerous viral diseases; tracheal mites – another, smaller, mite that lives inside the breathing tubes of the

24

bees; and, *Nosema apis/Nosema ceranae* – a pair of fungal infections of the bees digestive tract. The pest – small hive beetle also a major problem is some parts of the US.

Researchers at the University of Georgia report that a light dusting of up to a teaspoon of powdered sugar inside the hive will encourage bees to groom and will reduce *Verroa* levels.

In the authors experience, small hive beetle can quickly escalate from nuisance to an infestation sufficiently bad that the bees will abandon a hive. It has been suggested that #6 aluminum mesh, rather than solid bottom to the hive may help the bees manage the problem[12] (especially with a tray of cooking oil beneath to drown the beetles). A Google/Yahoo!/etc search will return several DIY traps using recycled corrugated plastic signs, vegetable shortening and boric acid that may work (or be adapted to work) in your hive.

FUN FACT
Honey has antibacterial and anti-fungal properties and has been used to treat infections since the time of the Pharaohs.

12 http://www.greenbeehives.com/abgrbe.html

Other Problems

Possibly because the top bars only support comb along the top edge, the author has found heavily laden comb occasionally detaches from a top bar during a heatwave. Also, while the top bars provide a guide for the bees to follow when building comb, and their width should dictate one comb per bar, try to not be too upset if your bees choose not to conform and surprise you with a two-bar comb – it's part of the fun!

FUN FACT
Honey consists of 35% fructose, 30% glucose, 18% water, 12% other sugars and 5% minerals/amino acids/proteins/etc.

Autumn (Fall)

Your first year hive is unlikely to be full, but in an exceptional year this would be the time to smoke the hive and remove a bar or two of comb furthest from the brood. It might also be a good idea to use an entrance reducer to prevent mice and other beasties setting up home with your bees.

Honey Extraction

Have replacement top-bars available to replace any you remove. Smoke the hive well and remove the comb you have selected for harvesting. Quickly place it in a food safe bag or storage tub.

Do not extract honey near the hive.

Once away from the hive, **and the bees**, the comb can be placed in an appropriate container and cut from the top bar and crushed until there are no whole comb cells. This mixture can now be separated by filtering through one or more metal sieves.

Wax Extraction

Once your honey has drained from the crushed comb, the beeswax be purified[13]. One simple method is to place a heat resistant bucket under the sieve and poor boiling water over the comb – the wax will melt leaving much of the detritus behind. As the water cools, the wax will harden, and the

---

13 There won't be much – typically less than 1 oz. per top bar.

process can be repeated adding a finer sieve layer such as an old cotton pillowcase. Beeswax is flammable, so using hot water to melt it is much safer than a naked flame!

Medication

If you feel the need to do preventative treatments for *Nosema* with Fumagilin-B, or treat for *Verroa* with an appropriate miticide, now would be a good time – after you have extracted any honey and before it gets too cold.

Always follow manufacturer instructions when using chemicals in your hives.

Bee Food – Autumn

As winter approaches, the hive needs stores of food. If you have extracted honey, or the stores seem slim, or just 'because', feeding is often appropriate.

Syrup

Traditionally a 2 sugar : 1 water is used in Fall, however as noted earlier there are advocates for 5:3 or 2:1 year around.

Winter

Keep the hive entrance and any ventilation holes clear of snow and ice.

Bees do not hibernate. When it is too cold to forage (below 54–57°f), the hive colony will form a cluster within the hive and will attempt to keep themselves warm. Bees at the outer edge will take a spell insulating their sisters before being replaced after a time by a less chilled coworker. All will vibrate their wings generating heat to maintain 92°f at the center of the cluster. The bees will subsist their honey stores. In especially cold environment you might consider a wind-break or shelter to protect the hive, or wrapping your hive with some form of insulation.

As bees deplete their honey stores, the cluster will move as a whole towards the front or back of the hive. The bees will probably not reverse their direction while in cluster, so it is best to determine the direction of travel early (when you can inspect the hive without freezing the bees or yourself) and rearrange their storage combs to all be in the direction of travel. If stores are running low, you may have to supply supplemental syrup or other food until spring brings fresh nectar. Sugar syrup is much cheaper than buying new bees!

In general there should be little to do with the bees in winter – take the time to read another bee book and learn something new. It's a good time to repair any damaged or worn equipment and assemble any new hives.

Bee Food – Winter

Winter feeding bees in top-bar hives can be problematic. There is rarely access from above as with Langstroth type hives and the bees are often not sufficiently active for entrance feeders (outside the hive) to be effective, and those placed inside require frequent opening of the hive to refill. The most effective solution is probably a frame feeder, but given the non-standard nature of top-bar hives these are not available off-the-shelf, and each bee keeper basically has to custom build their own.

A type of entrance feeder with an extended "feed trough" that passes into the hive, and uses a plastic soda bottle as a reservoir, can sometimes be used if the landing board and hive entrance are sufficiently aligned. These can be found quite cheaply on eBay, and are certainly worth investigating, but it may take some experimenting to find the best compromise between bottle volume and reach into the hive space. A bigger bottle means fewer visits to refill, but generally means less of the feeder is inside the hive.

"Feed Trough" Entrance Feeder.

Another potential issue with external feeders (especially in winter) is that they can be tempting targets for raccoons and other wildlife.

Syrup

As for Autumn. Syrup may be poured or sprayed onto emptied comb, or placed in an entrance or custom frame feeder.

Fondant

- 4 parts white sugar (by volume)
- 4 parts 2:1 syrup (by volume)
- 3 parts water (by volume)

Stir the ingredients while heating gently – do not allow to boil. When all solids are dissolved or the mixture reaches about 240°f, beat the mixture while cooling to mix in air bubbles, and when thick pour into a mold. Thin sheets that can be hung between bars or from a spare top-bar would probably be useful. Fondant is probably what was used as the sugar plug for the queen cage you got with your bee package. It can be used year round for supplemental feeding.

 FUN FACT
Bees produce honey as a winter food store.

Epilogue
(the new spring)

As winter fades, your bees will become active again. The colony will try to boost its numbers to take advantage of the new year. Feeding 1:1 syrup will give them a good start as they start to forage for food.

Your new year of beekeeping will be much the same as your first however you will now also have to consider the amount of comb used/available for brood – so long as there is space to grow, the hive should not swarm, but consider how you will respond if there are signs that they might.

If you want to split the established hive (in effect, create the effect of a swarm), you can take a couple of bars of comb with fresh brood[14] (and the attending nurse bees) and a couple with honey and pollen and put these in a new hive body a couple of bars back from the front. Shuffle the bars forward in your established hive, adding the empty bars replacement at the back. With feeding and a little luck, the bees will build you a new queen, and you will have two hives this year.

Here's hoping you have healthy and productive hives.

---

14 If you see vertically oriented, peanut shaped queen-cells on a brood comb, that might be a good choice.

Appendices

Suggested Links

Transcript of a discussion regarding use top-bar hives.
http://www.ibiblio.org/pub/academic/agriculture/entomology/beeke
eping/general/management/top_bar_faqs/tbhf.html

Plans for building a Kenya-style top-bar hive.
http://www.bushfarms.com/beestopbarhives.htm

Information on the "Honey Cow" hive manufactured from
a 55-gallon drum.
http://www.velacreations.com/honeycow.html

LCBA (Ohio) Paper on winter wrapping (insulation) of
hives. Specific to Langstroth hives, but good background
information if you live in colder regions.
http://www.loraincountybeekeepers.org/PDF
%20Files/MakingWinterWraps.pdf

Discussions and photos of various ingenious frame feeder
designs.
http://www.navitron.org.uk/forum/index.php/topic,7561.0.html
http://www.biobees.com/forum/viewtopic.php?
t=9183&view=previous&sid=0fe907398d0de2b7c22c90fa95c9cbf9
https://hollamoor.wordpress.com/2011/08/06/top-bar-hive-feeder/

Honey harvesting guide.
http://www.topbarbees.com/index.php?
option=com_content&view=article&id=86:extracting-honey-from-t
op-bar-comb&catid=52:honey-production-in-top-bar-hives&Itemid
=70

Swarm Trapping

A swarm is normally a successful bee colony's attempt to reproduce. With Langstroth hives, beekeepers often attempt to prevent swarming by destroying queen cells. You can attempt this with a top-bar hive, but it goes against the "let the bees manage themselves" philosophy that is generally applied to top-bar beekeeping. If you just want the one hive, you can let your bees swarm and either allow them to fend for themselves, or call a local beekeeper to collect them when you see a swarm gathering. Another approach is to 'trap' the swarm and start another hive of your own. This is a more advanced topic than I wish to get into in this book, but I will provide the following overview as guidance for your research.

A swarm trap is a container you place where you think a swarm might gather that the bees see as a suitable potential new home. It does not trap the bees as such, they are free to come and go, but it does tend to stop the swarm straying too far.

Commercial traps are available, but Langstroth 5-frame nuc boxes, and small (21 in., 12 top-bar) top-bar hives are also commonly used. It is reported that all that is really required to trap European honey bees is a container with an internal volume of 30-40 liters (8-10 US gal.) with a roughly 15 cm^2 ($2^1/_3$ cu. in) entrance. Many beekeepers just build simple wooden boxes of appropriate dimensions.

If a non-slot type hole is used, it is a good idea to use a nail or wire to prevent larger creatures than bees taking up residence. Also, while smaller containers may work, they should be avoided in areas where the presence of Africanized bees is known, or even suspected. It has been suggested that these more aggressive bees prefer a 20-30 liter (5-8 US gal.) volume.

Traps are generally placed a few feet off the ground, to above head height, in locations where swarms are expected to pass by. The 'bait' is a drop or two of lemon-grass oil near the entrance, applied weekly, or a commercial lure used as directed. Commercial traps tend to need more frequent checking to avoid excessive comb build-out. Use of a small top-bar hive or top-bar compatible box is probably the easiest option for the top-bar beekeeper as the trapped swarm can be left to start building out comb, and the top-bars moved en mass to a new hive at a time more convenient to the beekeeper.

Credits

Text, photographs and drawings by Stephen Garriga except as follows:

- Photographs of the author working hives on pages 6 and 7 and cover photographs © 2012, Debra Anderson – used with permission;

- Honey bee glyph, farmer with skeps and queen, worker & drone woodcuts derived from images stated as public domain at http://www.clker.com;

- Swarm image, "Hive" by Bobby Mikul stated as public domain at http://www.publicdomainpictures.net.

Notes

24108856R20027

Made in the USA
Middletown, DE
14 September 2015